QR Interactive

Coloring Books ©

Congratulations! You have chosen a unique coloring book that will provide entertainment, reduce stress and leave you with a feeling of tranquility.

- Download a free "QR Reader" to your cellphone

- Scan the code on each page

A video will pop up showing you the motivation for the drawing.

The idea is to relax and have fun. That combination requires that you set the scene for a great artistic experience. Betty Edwards book, "Drawing from the right side of the brain" is about a shift. Moving from verbal to a hard-to-access "R" -mode, a place where words aren't needed. Basically going to "The Zone".

The Zone is a cool place. In golf, it's called "unconscious confidence". No thought. To get there you have to know everything, then forget it.

First, clear your plate. Take out the trash, do your homework, pay bills, whatever. Eliminate your barriers for a more lengthy session. The idea is quality. If you can spend (5) good minutes coloring that's great, (30) minutes in the coloring zone…even better.

Crayon • Colored Pencils • Marker • Ball Point Pen • Lead Pencil • Chalk

Try different methods, combine them, let your mind explore. Lay out your tools so you can grab the easily. Turn on some good music, have your favorite drink in arm's reach.

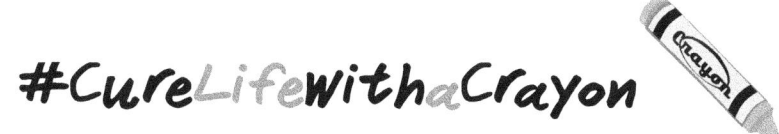

#CureLifewithaCrayon

Twist

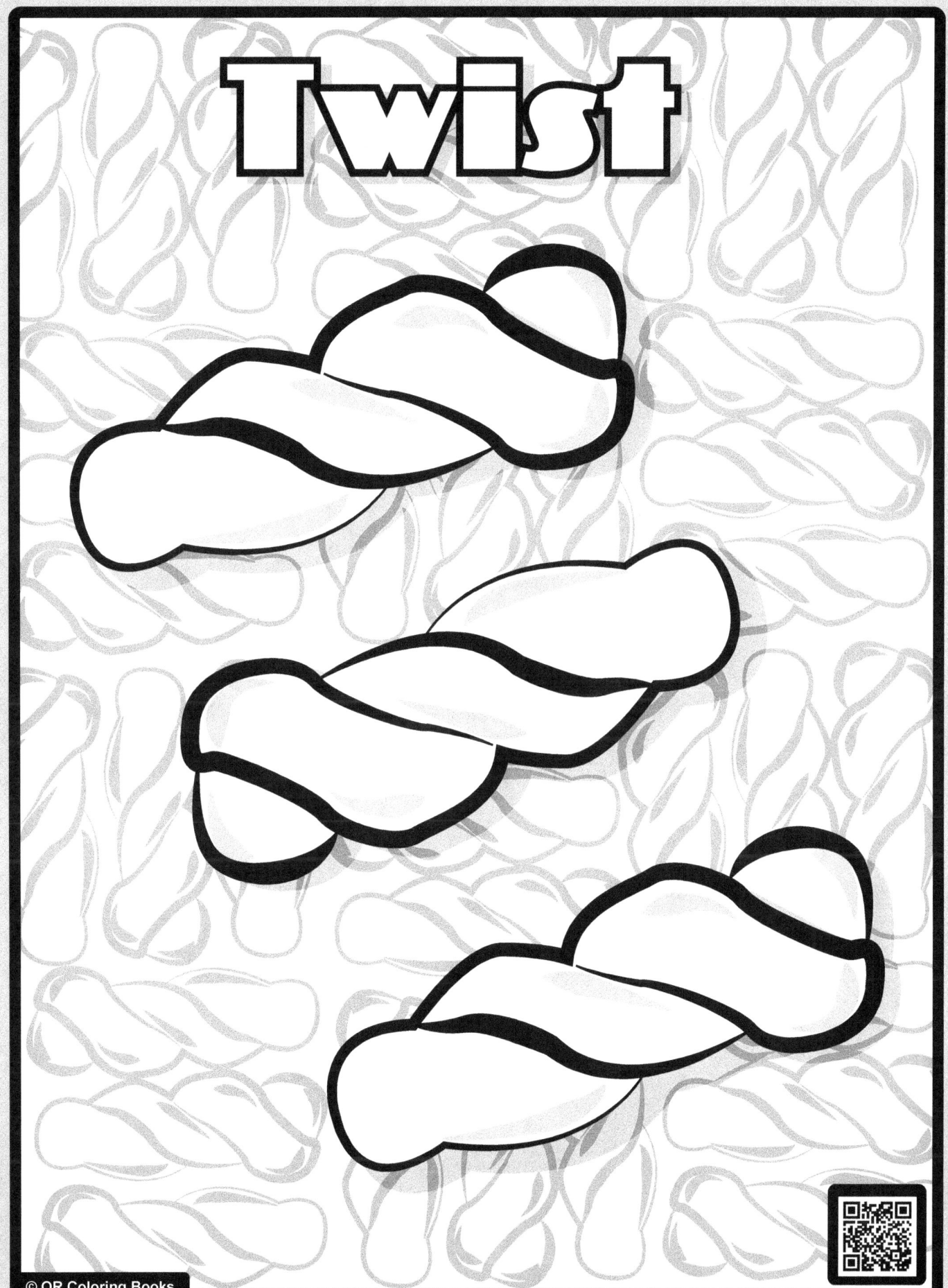

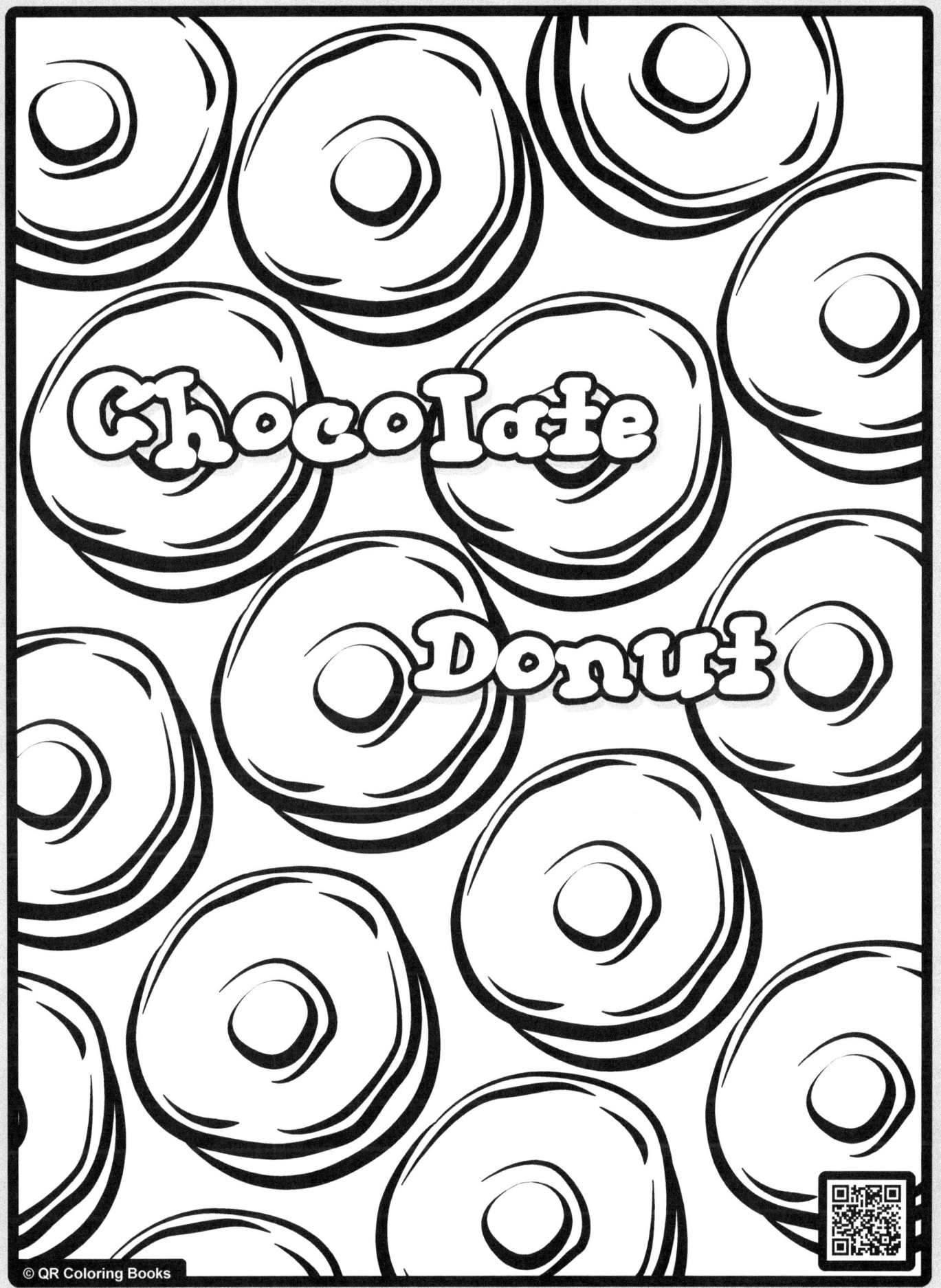

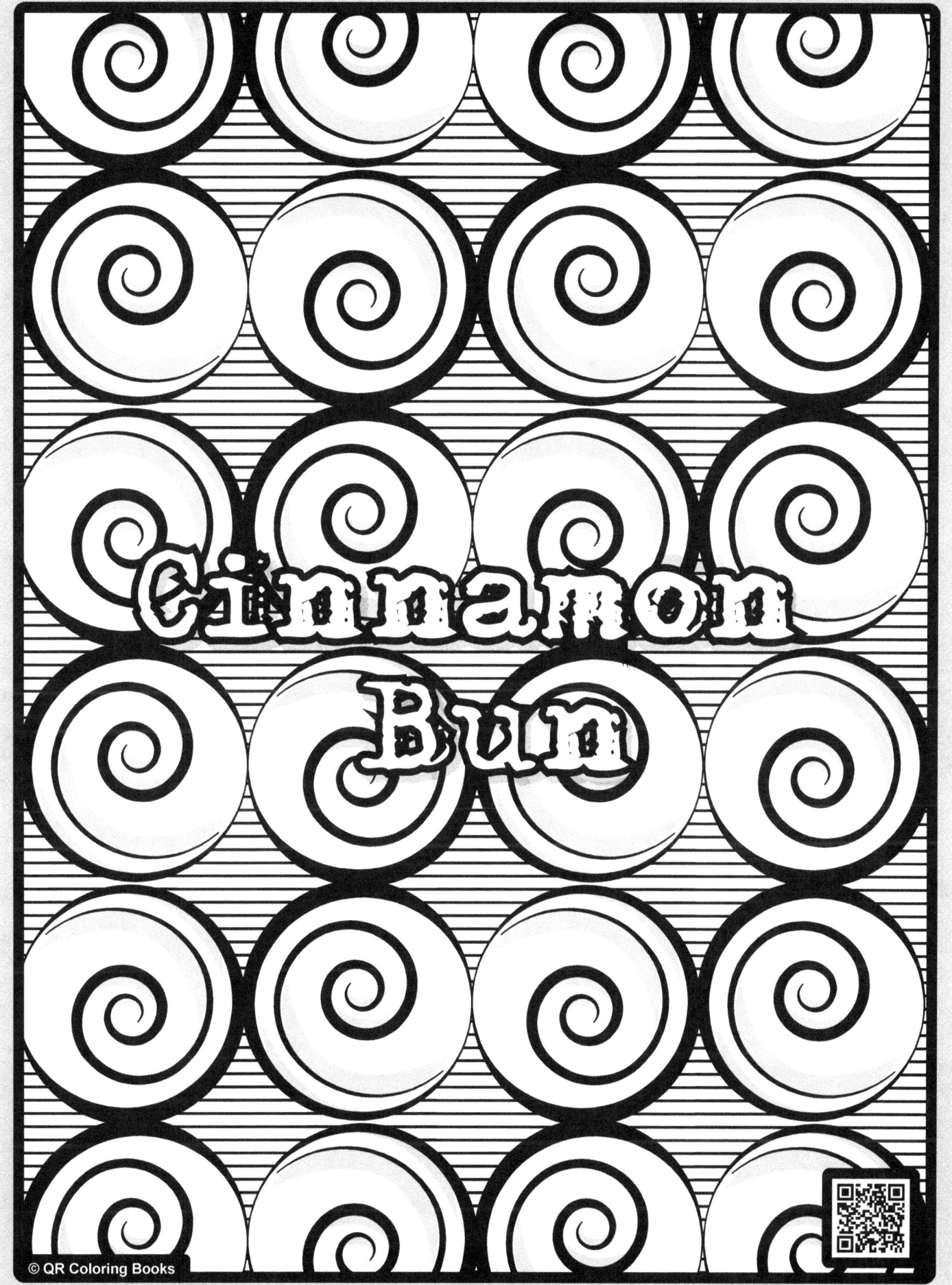

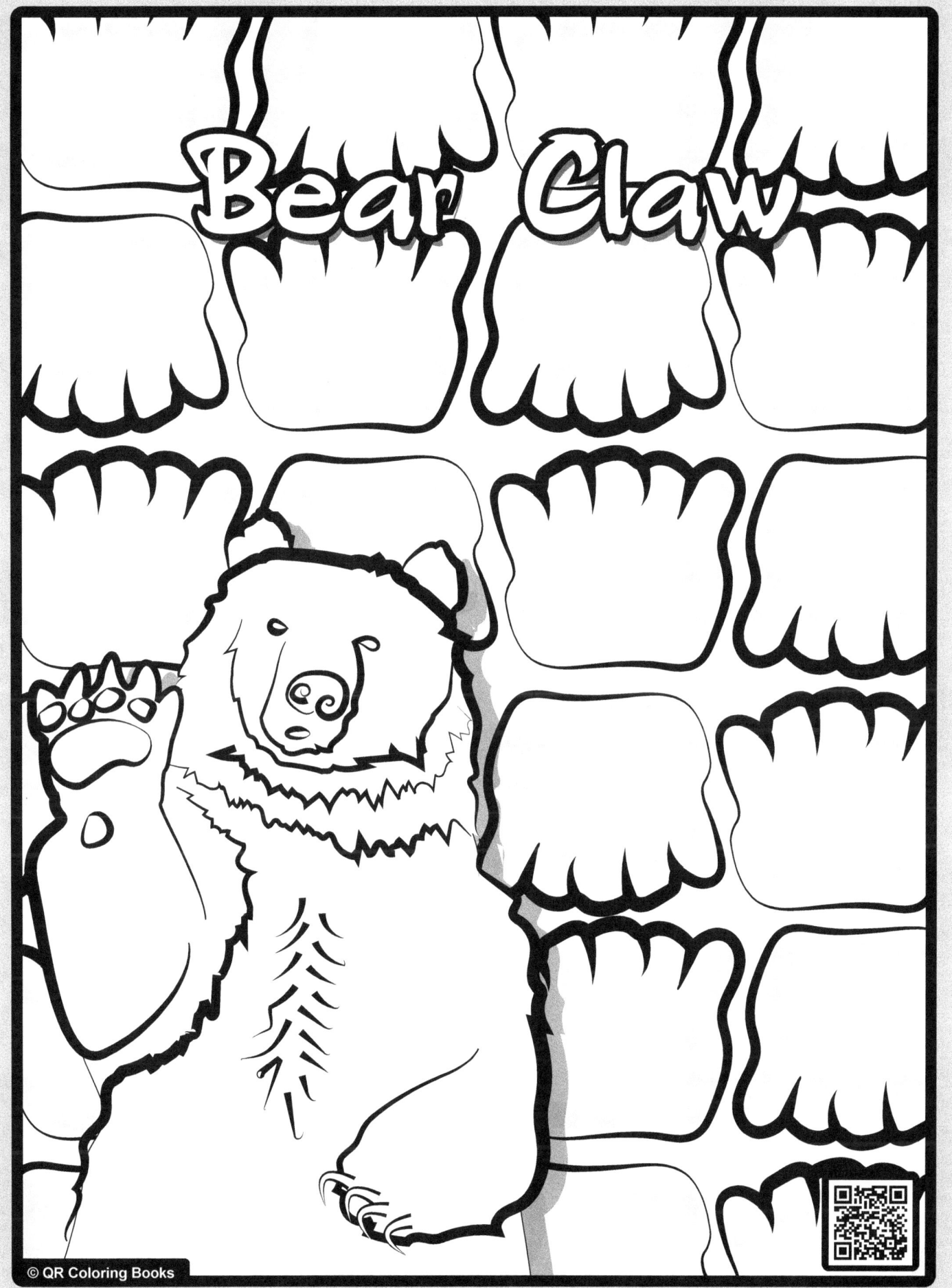

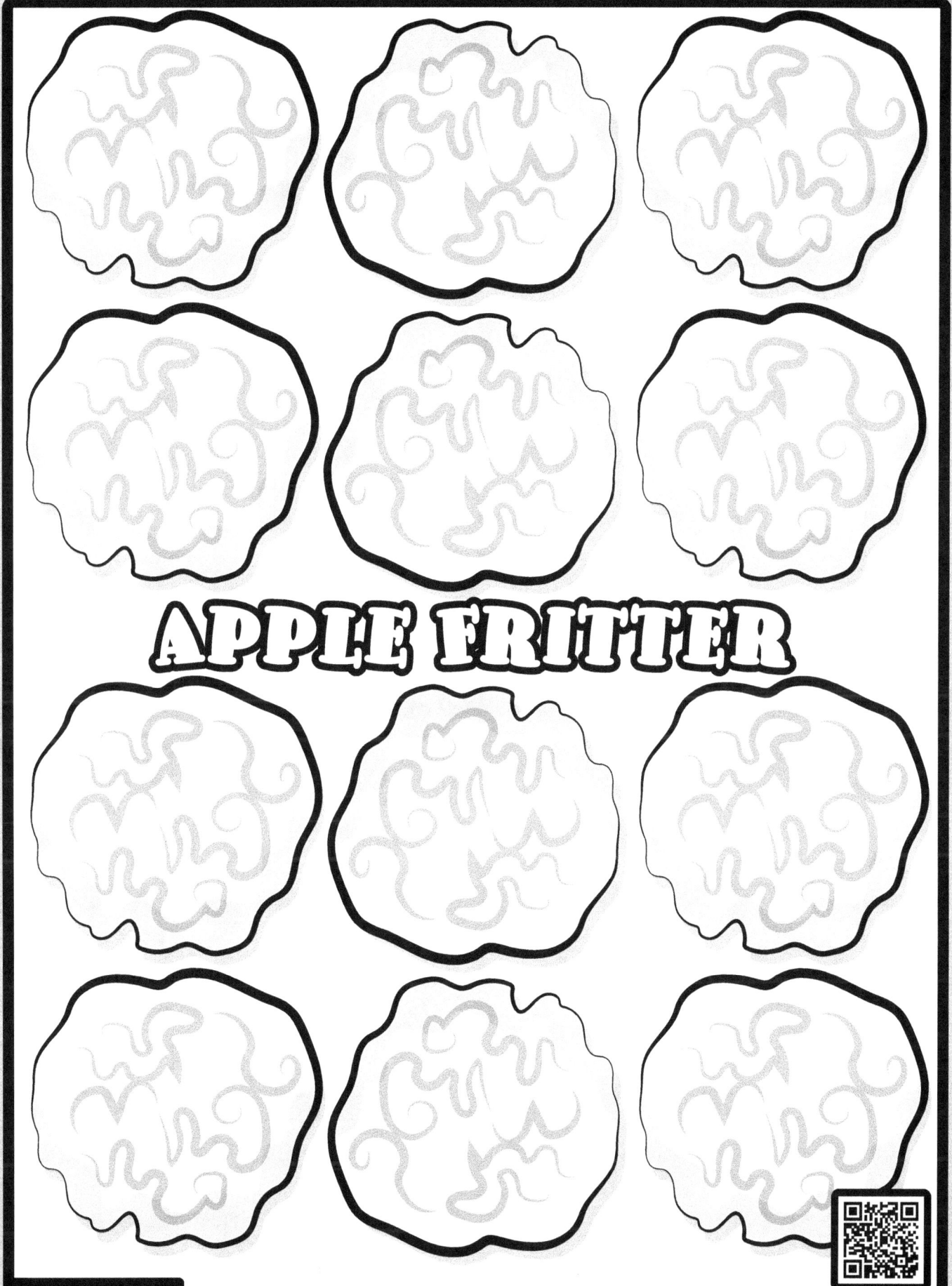

APPLE FRITTER

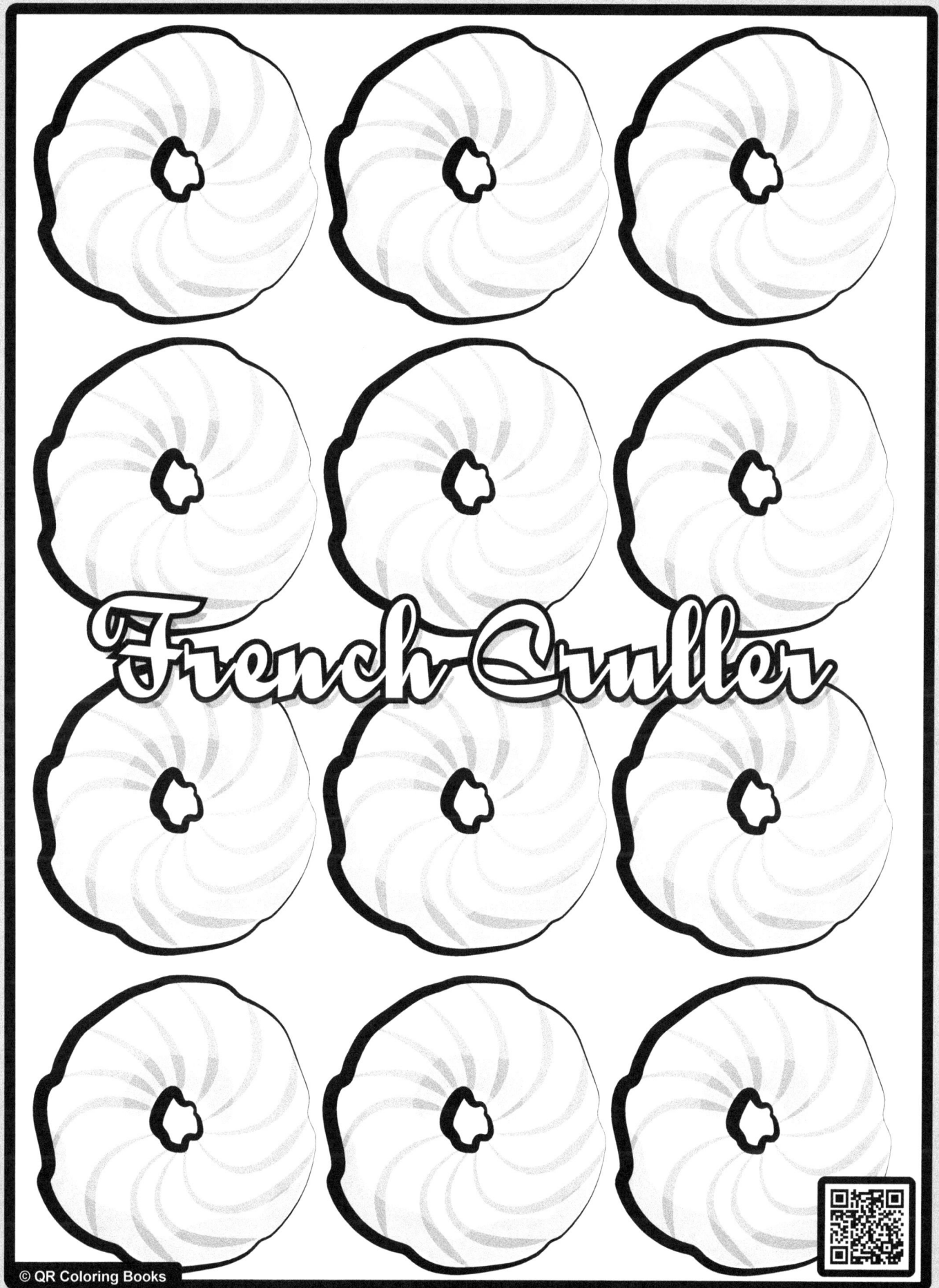

French Cruller

BOSTON CREAM

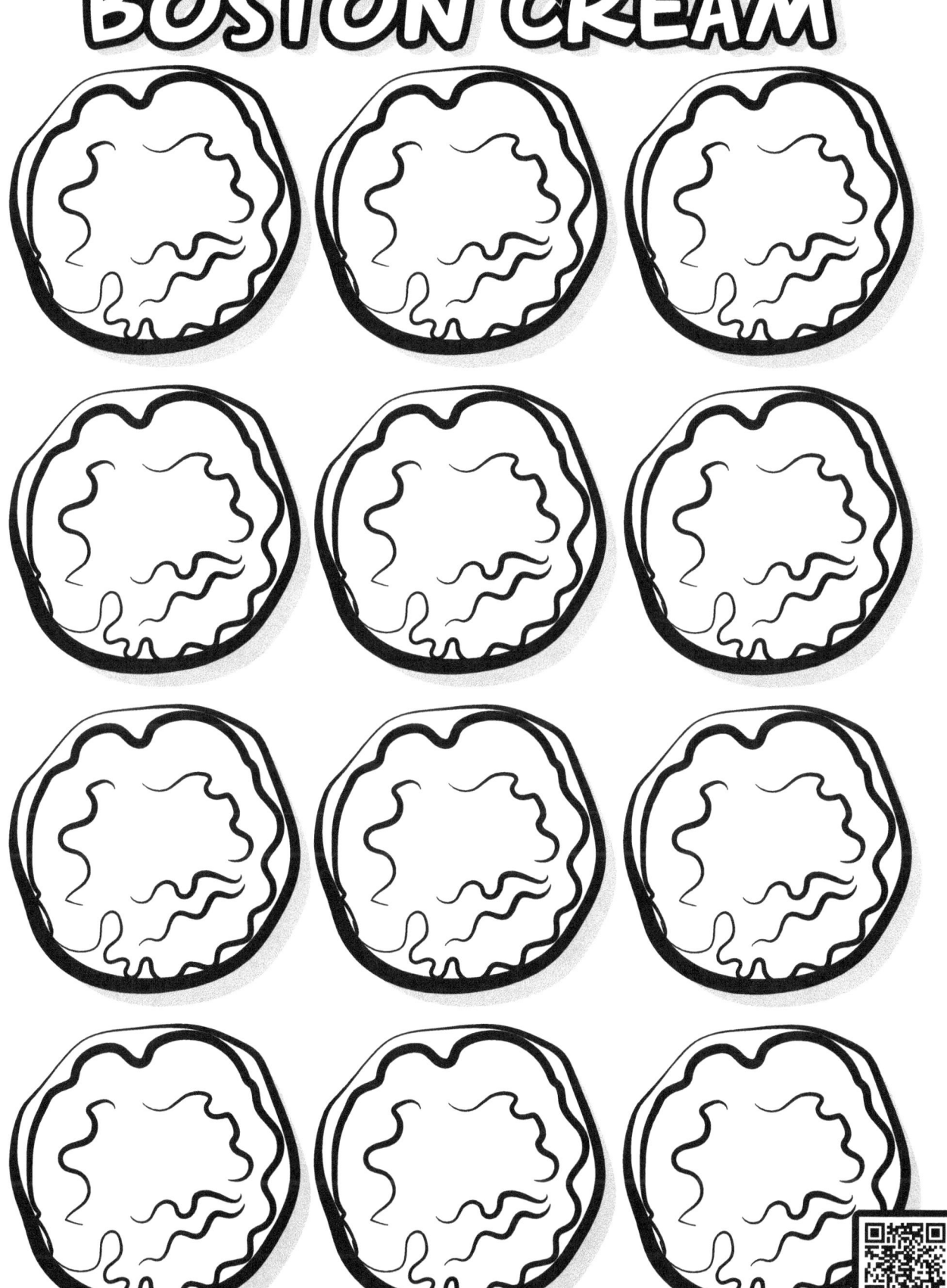

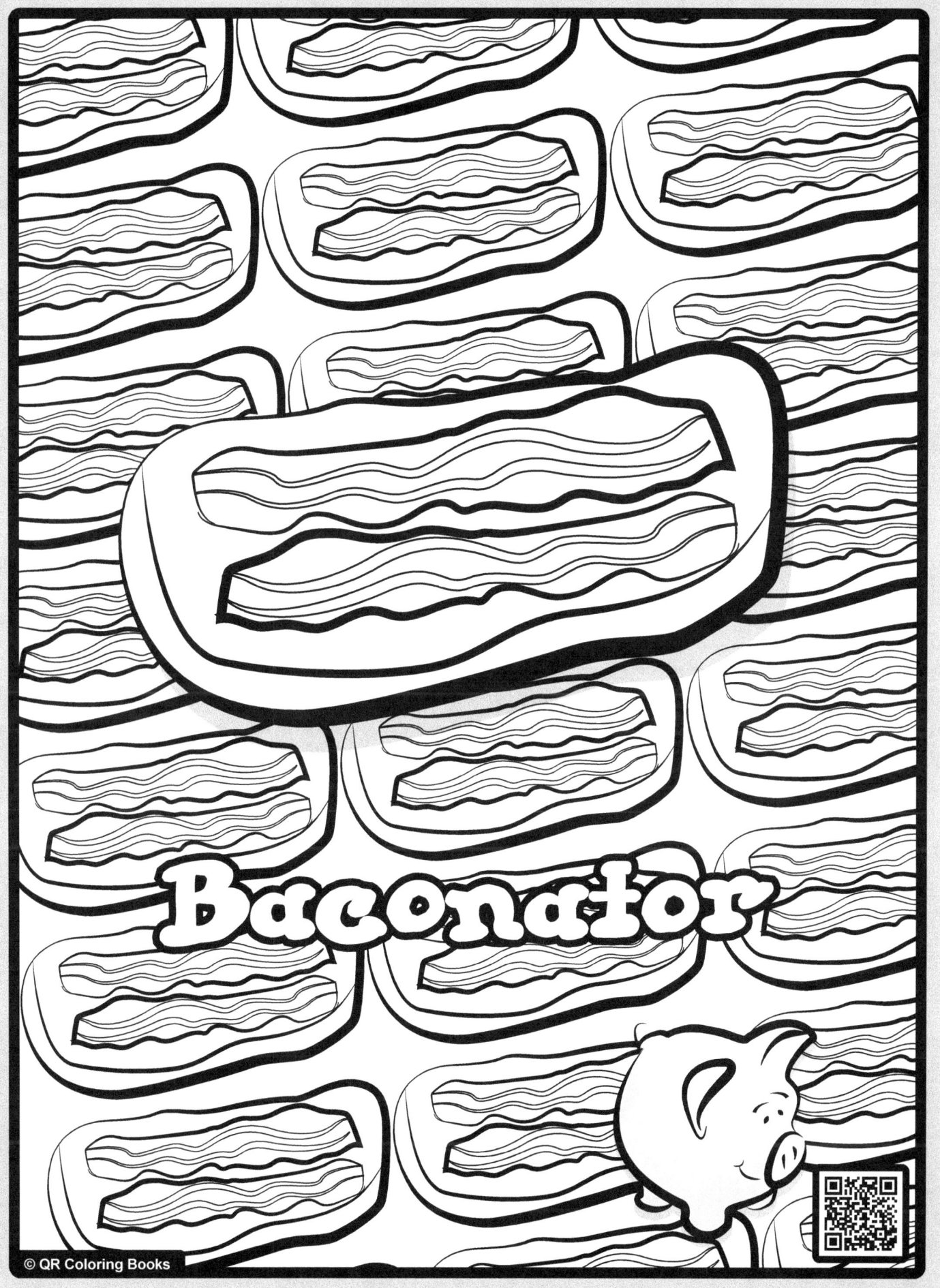

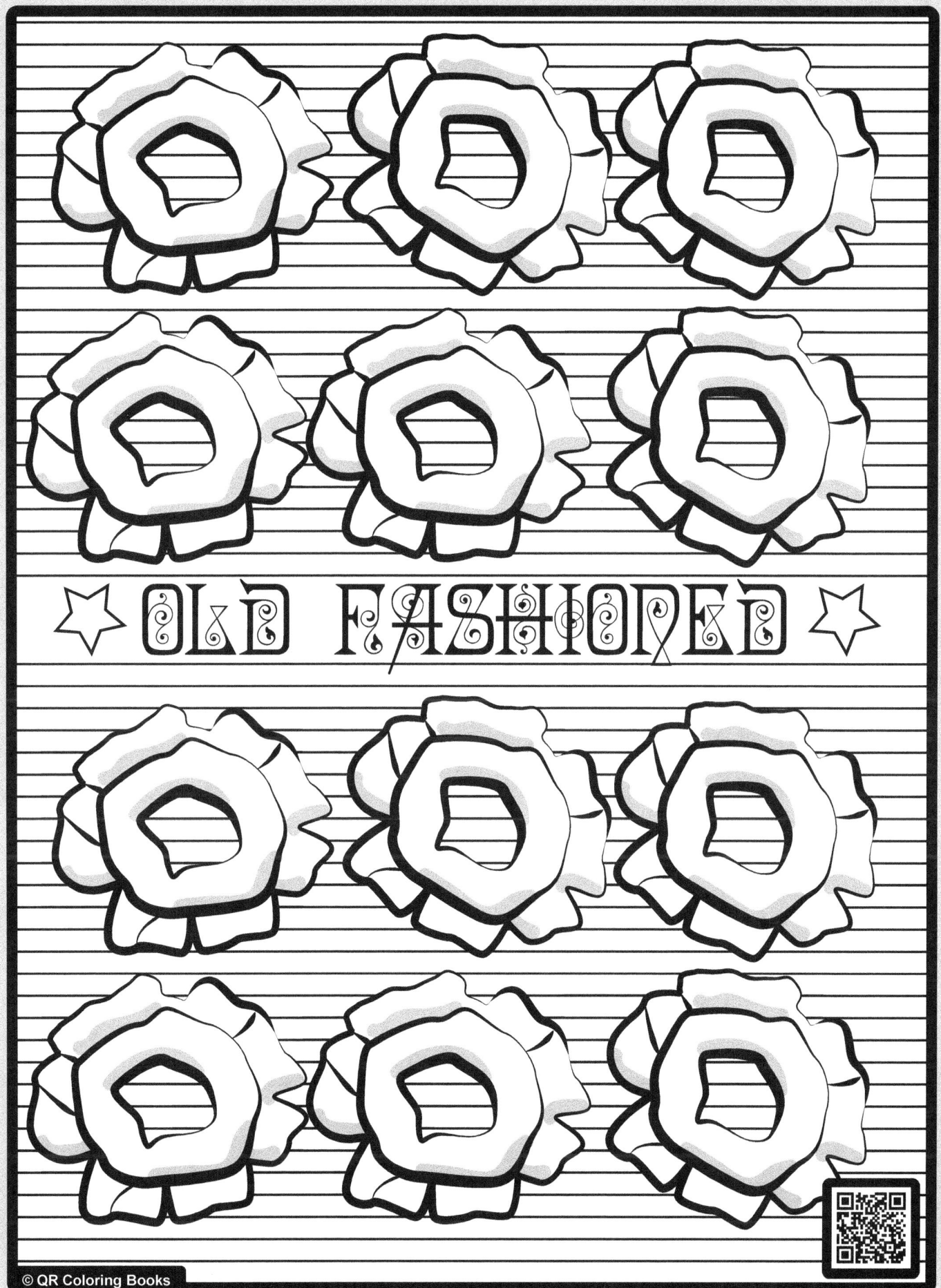

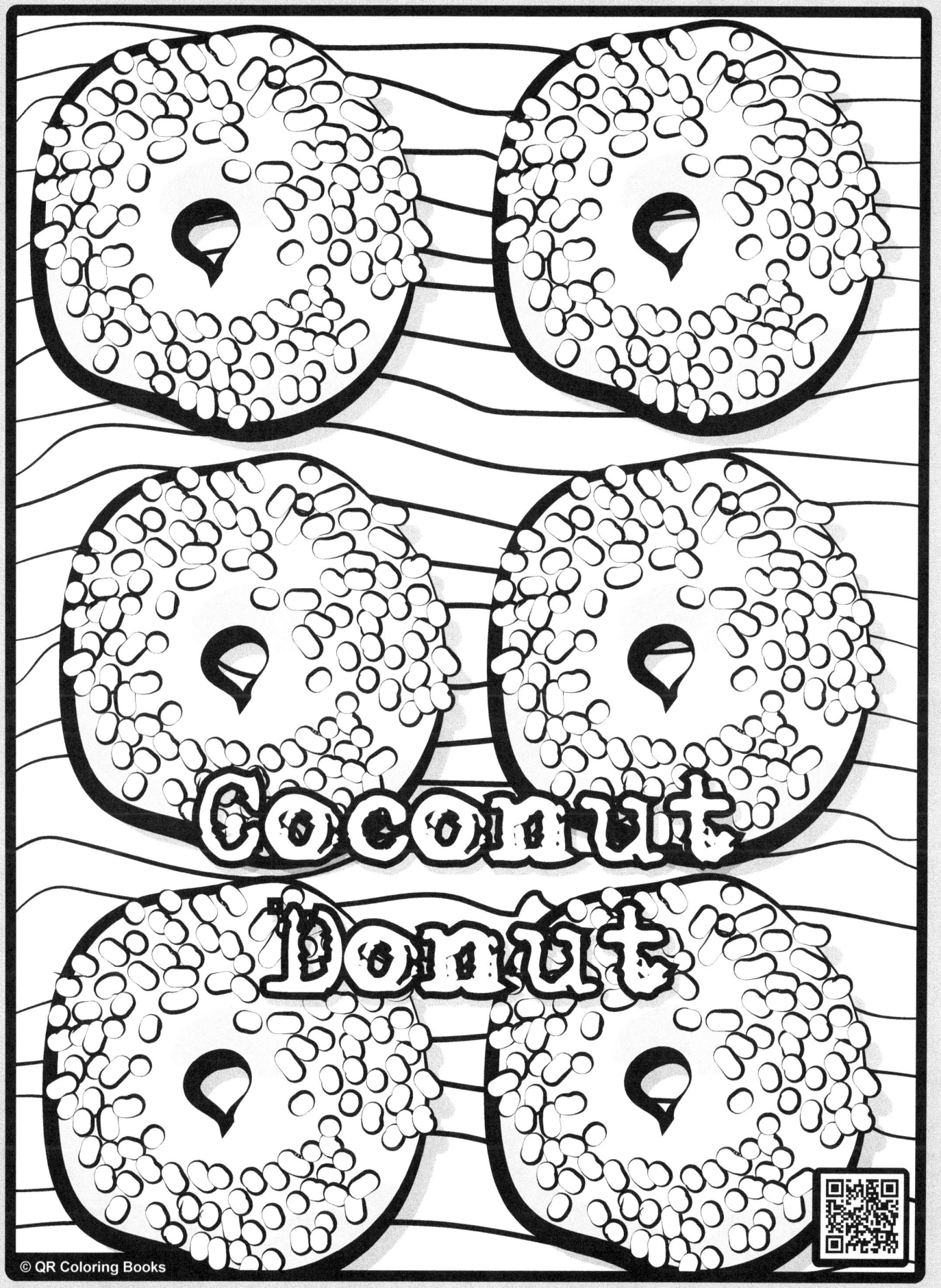

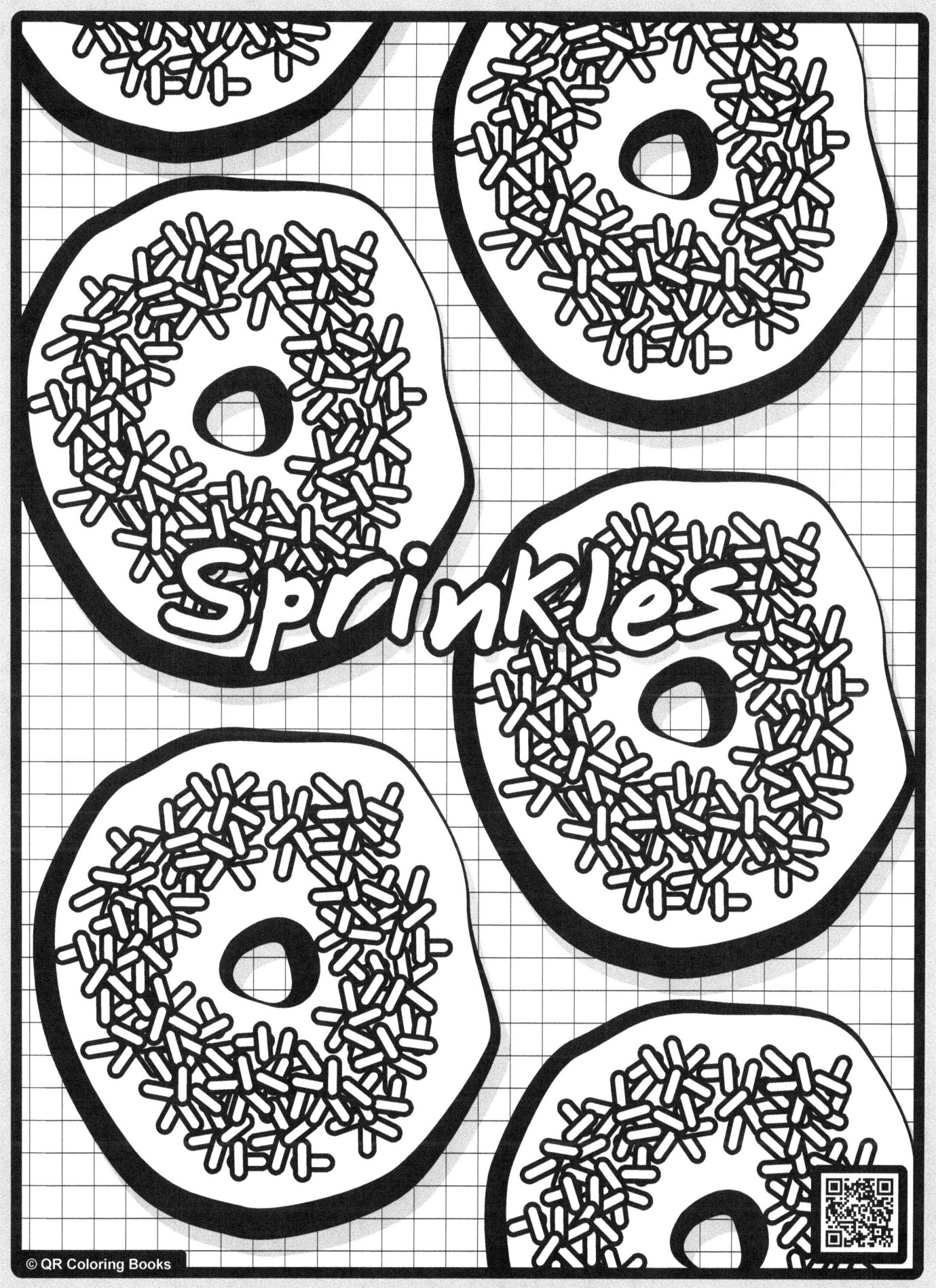

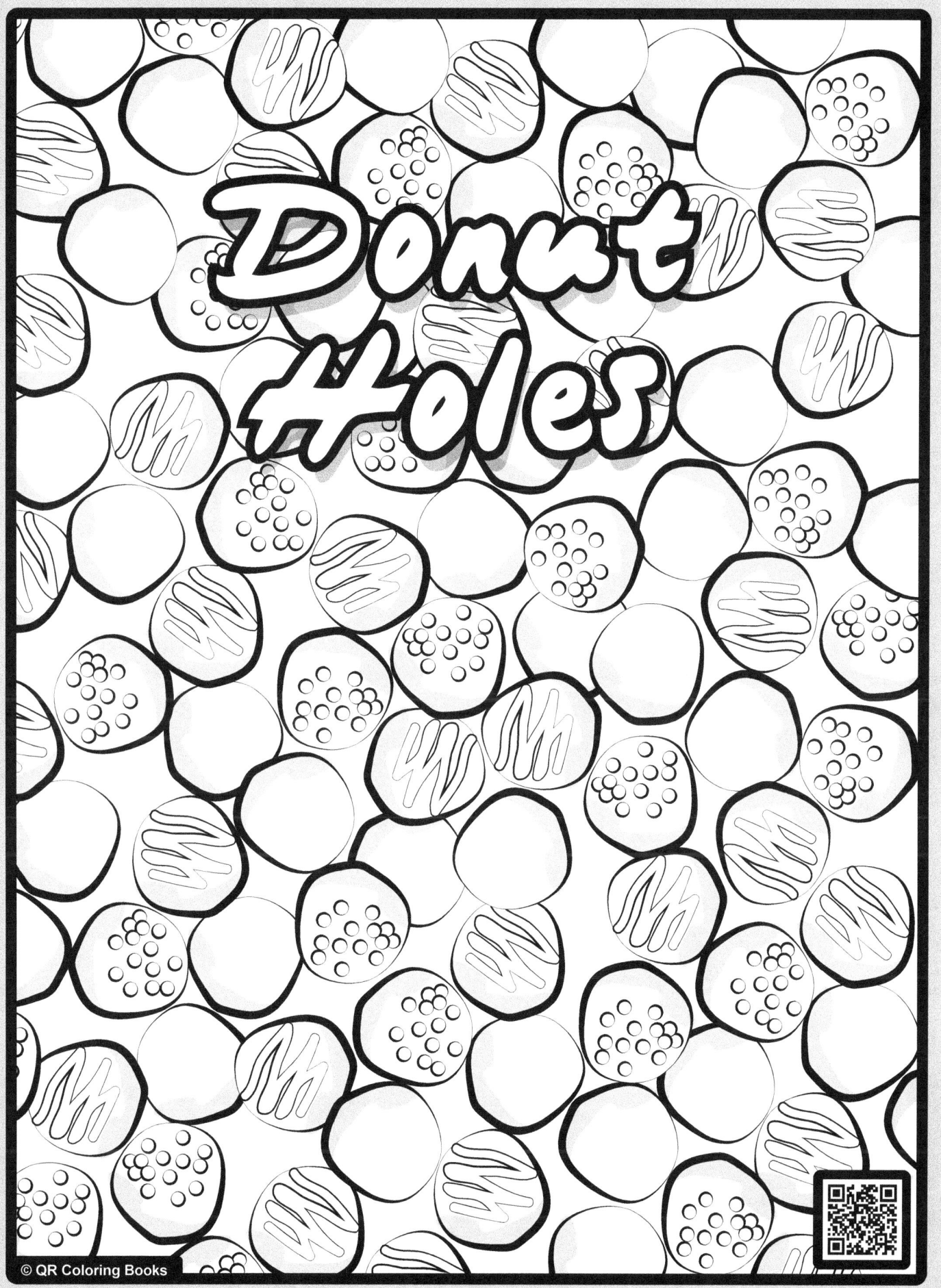

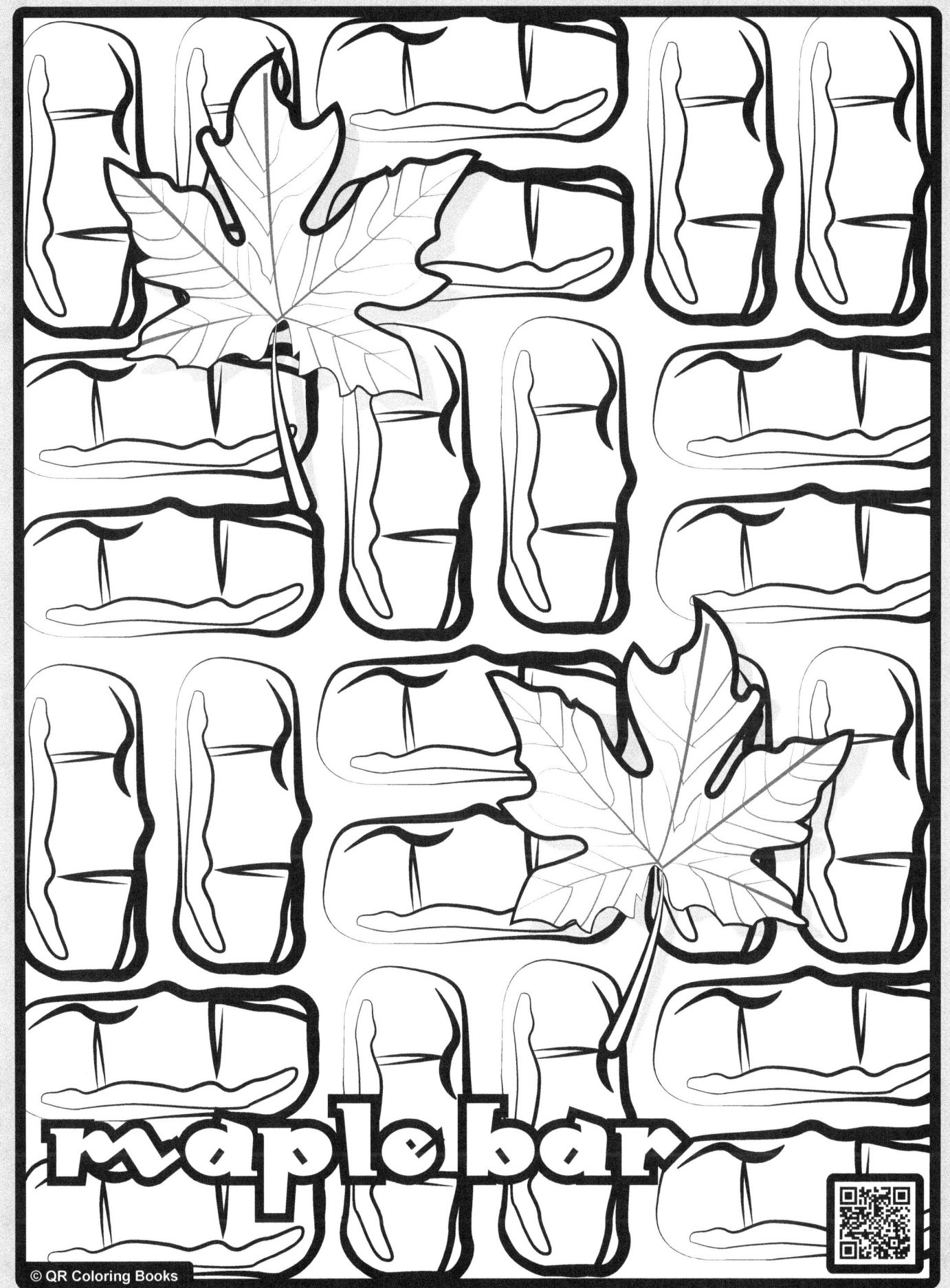

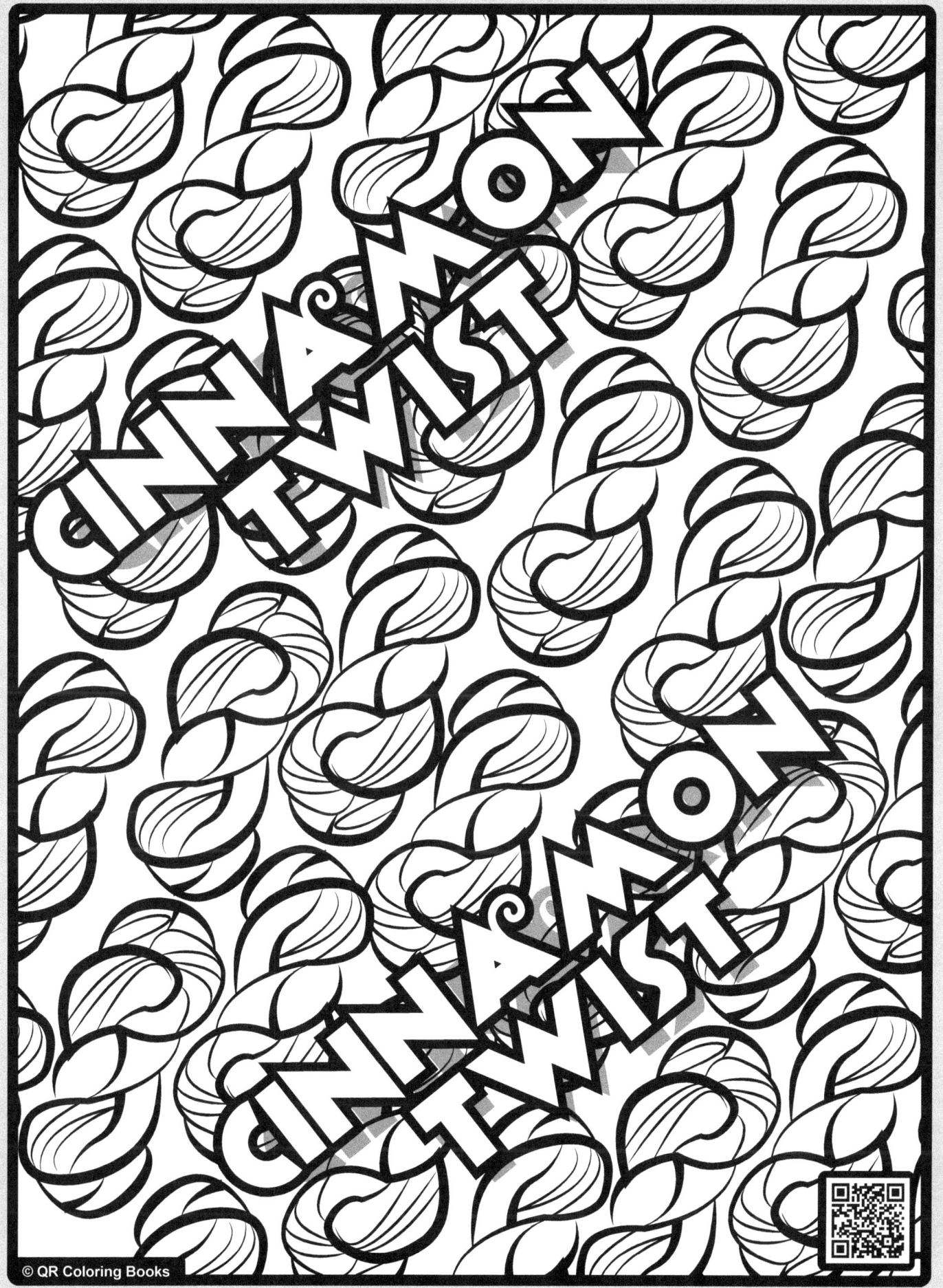

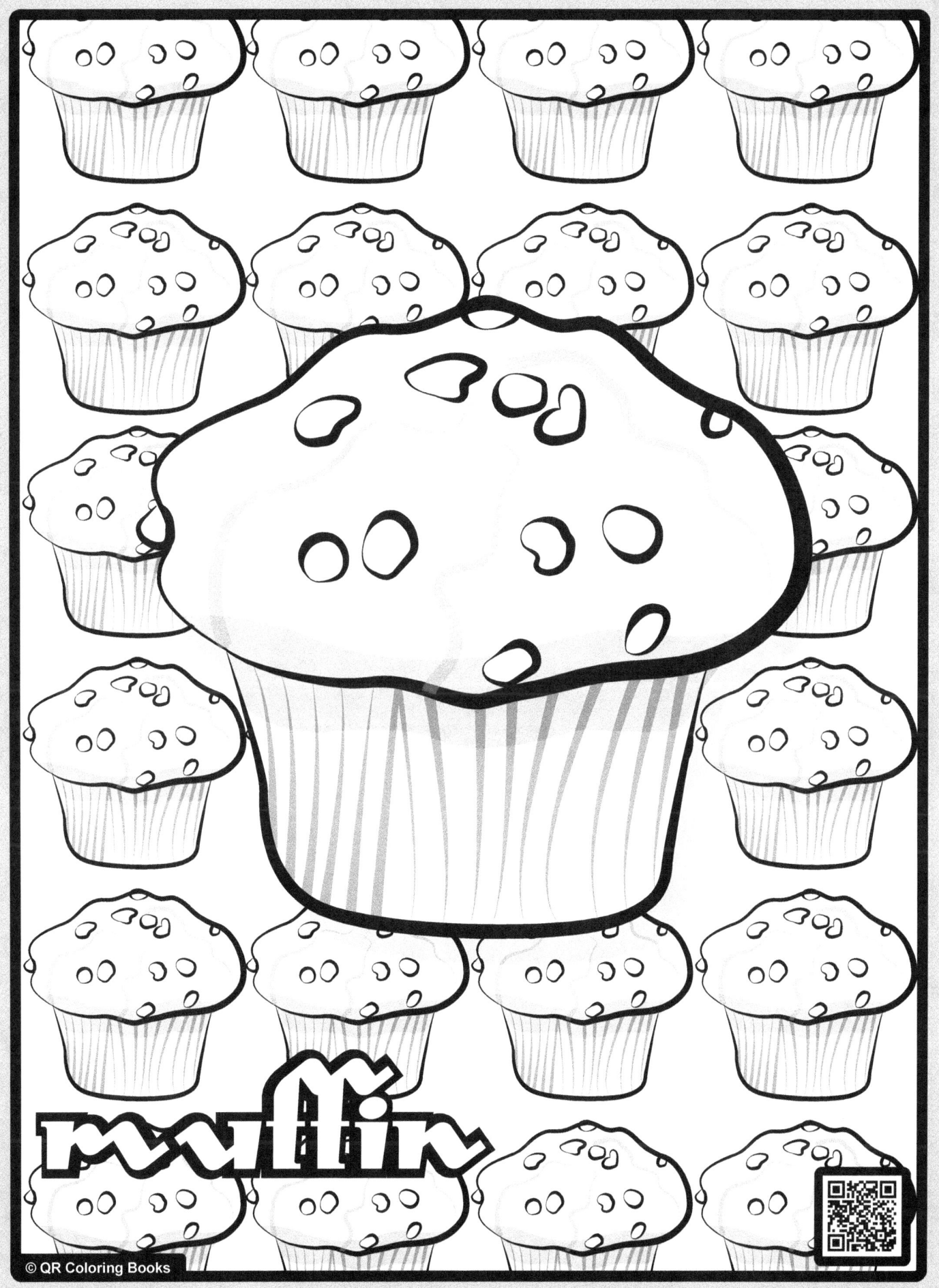

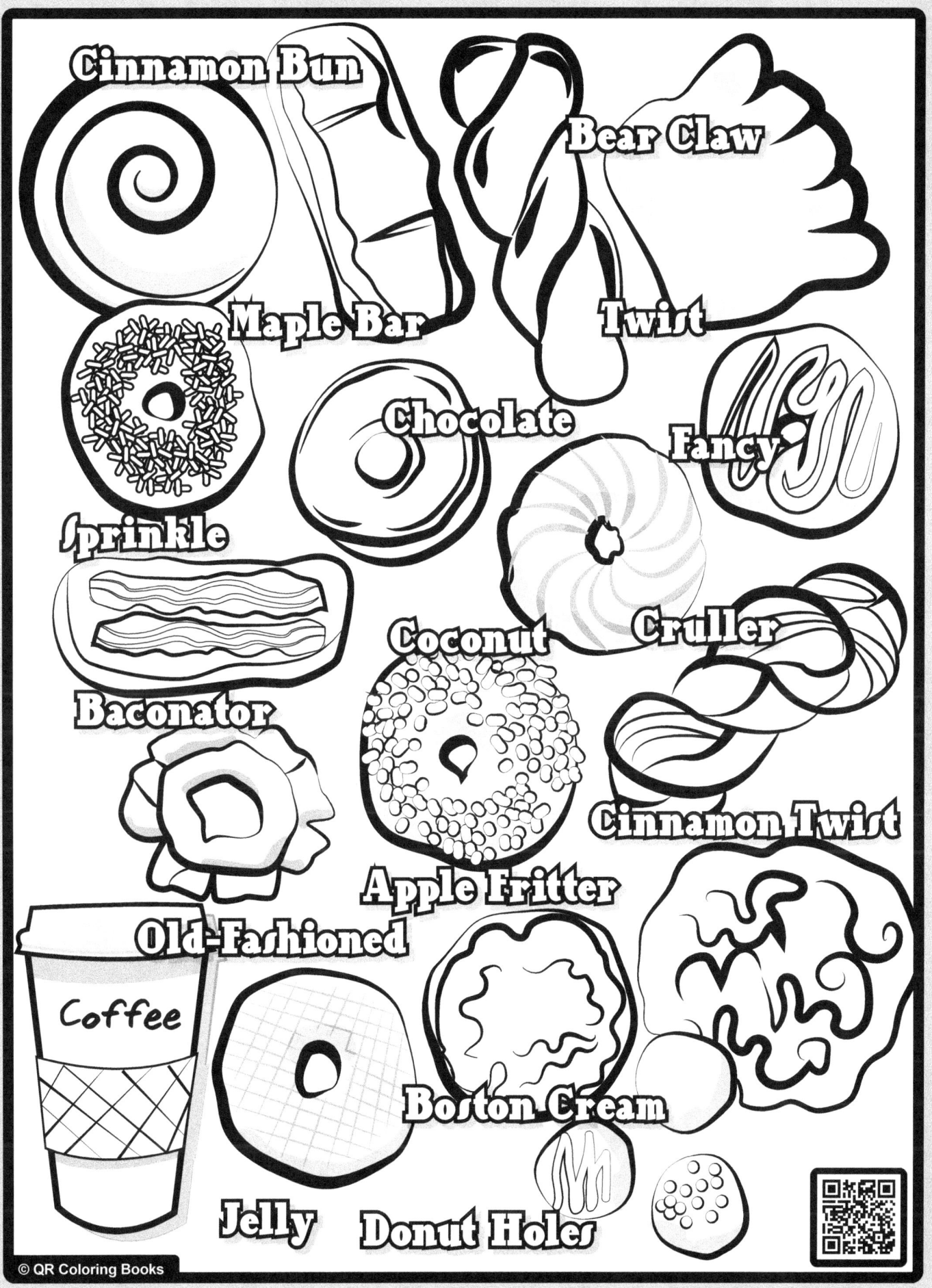

Cinnamon Bun

Bear Claw

Maple Bar

Twist

Chocolate

Fancy

Sprinkle

Cruller

Coconut

Baconator

Cinnamon Twist

Apple Fritter

Old-Fashioned

Coffee

Boston Cream

Jelly

Donut Holes

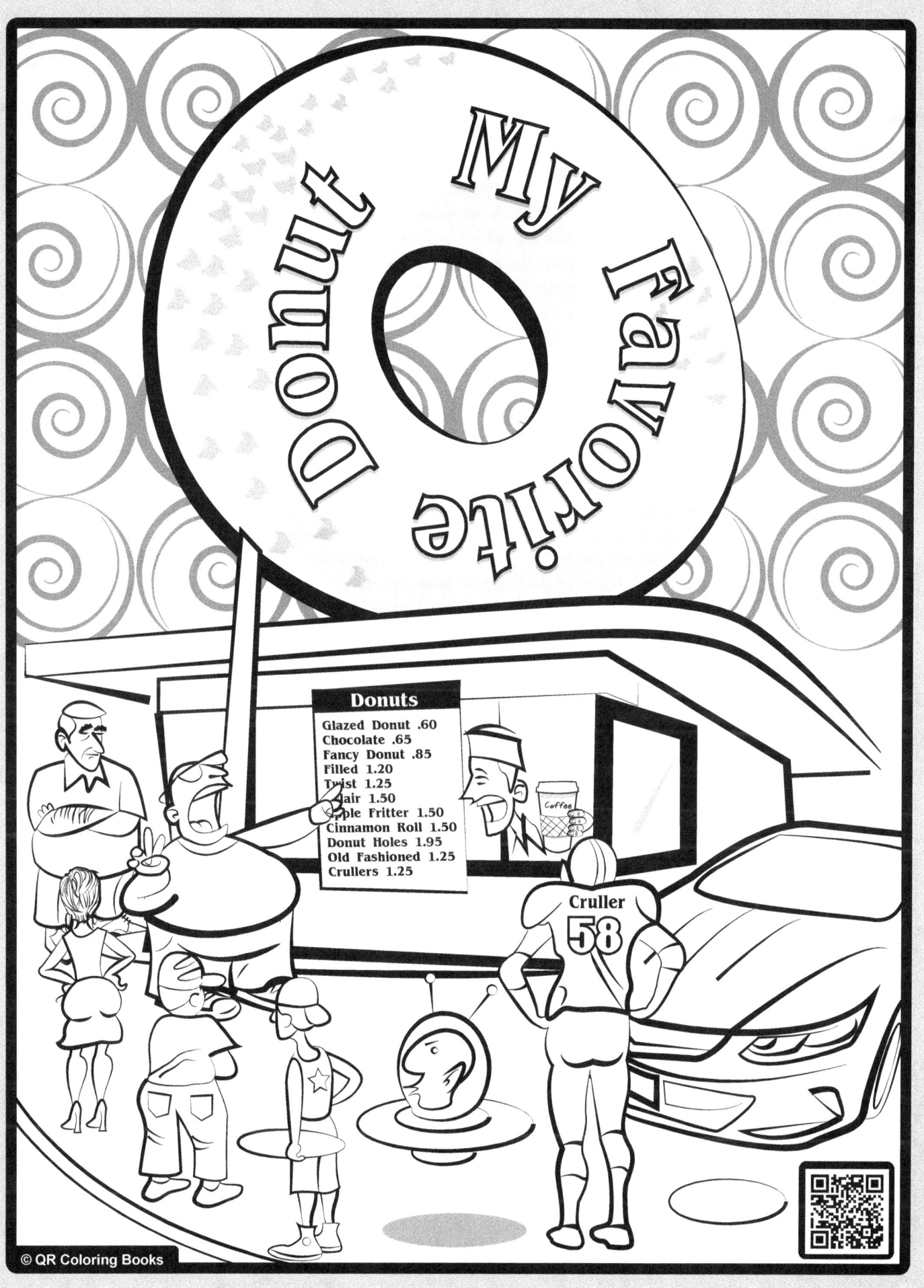

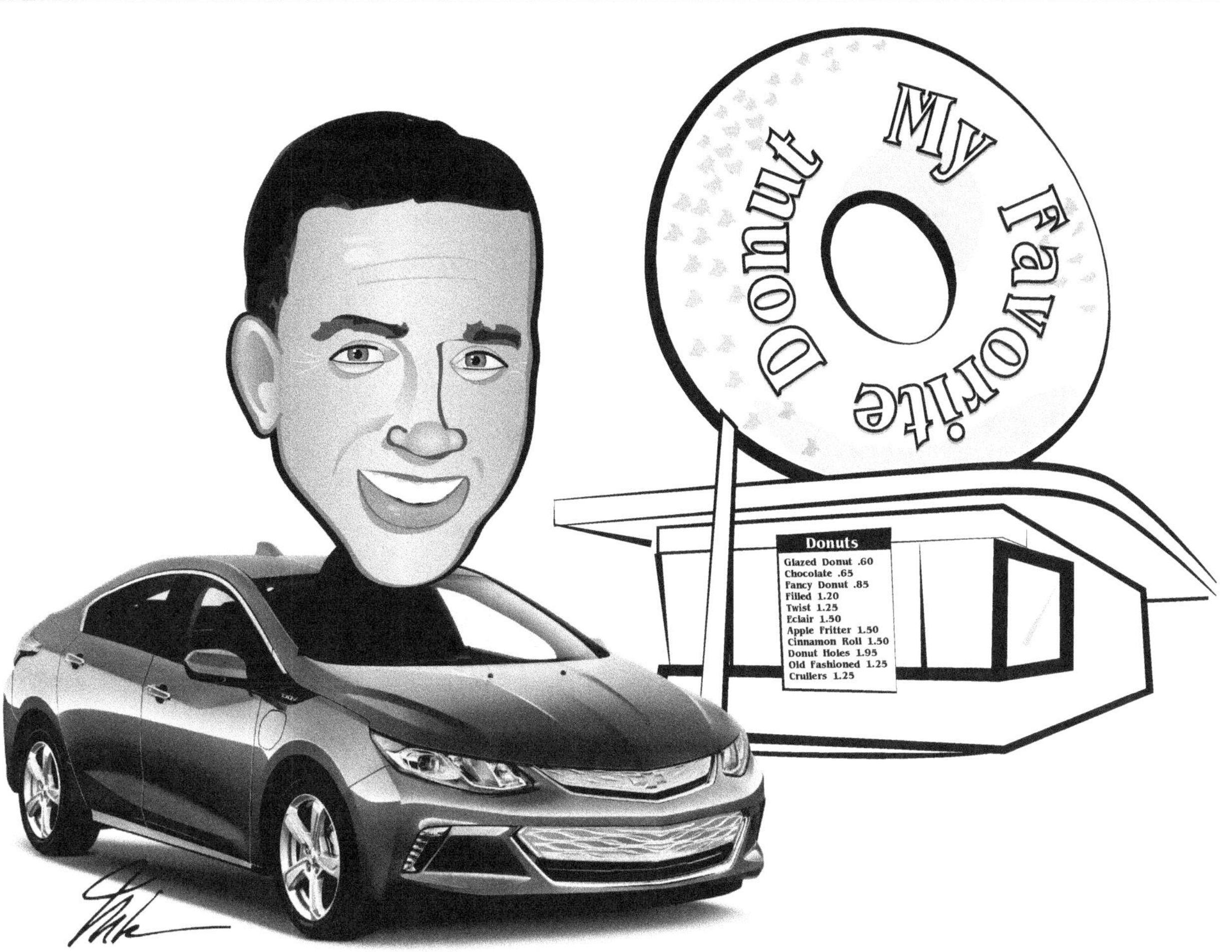

Donuts

Glazed Donut	.60
Chocolate	.65
Fancy Donut	.85
Filled	1.20
Twist	1.25
Eclair	1.50
Apple Fritter	1.50
Cinnamon Roll	1.50
Donut Holes	1.95
Old Fashioned	1.25
Crullers	1.25

My Favorite Donut

Created by:
Mike Browne

My favorite donut coloring book was created because of the pink box. When I was a teenager in my neighborhood there was a store called " Toluca Market" . At 2:00 am they would bake old-fashioned donuts that we would buy on the way home from the club for Sunday morning. We would camp out in the living room and watch football while chowing down on donuts and milk. That was years ago and a pleasant memory. If I do that too often now I will end up the shape of a pear or avocado.

Even worse mango.

Have fun coloring!

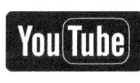